SMALL TOWN, BIG CITY......
A STORY WROTE BY DANIEL A. BROCK

BEGINNING:

IN A SMALL TOWN OF HARRISONSBURG OHIO, A SMALL SLEEPY GERMANIC TOWN ON THE OHIO AND INDIANA BORDER, EVERYBODY KNOWS EVERYBODY SETTING...

THE FRIENDLY TOWN HAS THE USUAL SHOPS AS ANY OTHER SMALL COMMUNNITY TOWNS... THE MAIN STREET GOING THROUGH THE TOWN WAS NAMED SPRINGLEAF AVENUE.. OTHER SIDE STREETS TO NAME A FEW WAS 1ST, 2ND, 3RD STEETS AND MORE.. MOM" & POP STORES, GIFT SHOPS, HOME COOKING RESTURANT CALLED " PARTONS FAMILY DINNING " . THE MAIN PLACE TO TAKE THE FAMILY OUT TO DINNER. WELL KNOWN FOR THEIR DUTCH APPLE PIE.. DOWN ON THE CORNER JOHN'S GAS & GROCERY..

THE SCHOOLS " HARRISONBURG ELEMENTARY, HARRISONBURG MIDDLE & HARRISONBURG HIGH, WHICH THE SPORT TEAMS WERE CALLED THE HARRISONBURG " TIGERS "... THE FOOTBALL TEAM WAS LEAGUE CHAMPIONS, AND ONE OF THE BEST IN THE STATE.

ON JULY 5TH 1981 BRAD COLLINS WAS BORN IN TO STEVE & SARA COLLINS IN HARRISONBURG COMMUNITY HOSPITAL.

ON DECEMBER 20TH 1981 MARIA JOHNSON WAS BORN TO DAVID & SUE COLLINS AT THE SAME HOSPITAL.

BRAD AND MARIA BECOME FRIENDS AS SOON AS THEY WERE BOTH PUT IN KINDER GARDEN AND BEYOND.
BRAD'S PARENTS BECAME FRIENDS WITH MARIA'S PARENTS, THEY HAD FAMILY GET TOGETHERS, DINNERS, COOK OUTS, SCHOOL ACTIVITES..

BRAD AND MARIA WERE UNSEPERABLE, THEY WERE , WELL SIMPLY PUT BEST FRIENDS. FROM THE TIME THEY WAS 5 YEARS OLD

ONE DAY A GENTELMAN AND JUDO EXPERT FROM THE EAST COAST NAMED CARL BROWN MOVED NEAR THE TOWN AND OPENED UP A JUDO SCHOOL..

RIGHT AWAY THE PARENTS OF BOTH CHILDREN, HEARD AND SAW THE SCHOOL OPENING SOON, SO THEY DECIDED TO GO TO THE GRAND OPENING WITHIN A COUPLE WEEKS..

WEEKS WENT BY THEN ON A LATE SUMMER SATURDAY AFTERNOON IN 1988 ,THE DOORS OPENED, MR. BROWN HAD A GREAT TURNOUT, HAD MUSIC, DOOR PRIZES, GIFTS, FOOD, CUPCAKES AND PIZZA..YOU NAME IT THEY HAD IT ALL..

MR. BROWN HAD 25 OR MORE STUDENTS TO JOIN AND SOME OTHER ADULTS AS WELL FROM THE TOWN AND NEIGHBORING TOWNS AND CITIES..

THE PARENTS OF BRAD AND THE PARENTS OF MARIA SIGNED THEM UP.
THEY WERE BOTH THE TENDER AGE OF 7. THEY NEVER MISSED A LESSON THEY PRACTICED TOGETHER... THE KIDS CLASS WAS CALLED " LITTLE WARRIORS " PROGRAM..

BRAD AND MARIA ATTENDED THE SAME ELEMENTARY SCHOOL AND OFTEN PLAYED IN SCHOOL PLAYS AND MUSICALS..

THE ONE THING THAT MARIA'S PASSION WAS OF COLLECTING OF STUFFED DOGS FORGET DOLLS, SHE LOVED DOGS, HER ROOM WAS FILLED WITH ALL KINDS OF STATUES OF DOGS AND STUFFED ANIMAL DOG AND TOY DOGS..

SHE ALWAYS WOULD SLEEP WITH ONE OF HER MANY STUFFED ANIMAL DOGS INSTEAD OF A TRADITIONALLY AMERICAN GIRL LIKING A TEDDY BEAR OR DOLL....

HER FAVORITE TOY DOG WAS A BLACK AND WHITE DOG SHE NAMED " PATCHES "

THE REASON MARIA NEVER HAD A REAL LIFE DOG IS BECAUSE SADLY SEE WAS ALLERGIC TO DOGS...BUT LATER GREW OUT OF THE ALLERGIC REACTION.

MARIA HAD TWO OLDER SIBLINGS JESSICA AND FRANK " FRANKIE " WAS THE OLDEST, PLAYED FOOTBALL BIG FOR HIS AGE, JESSICA WAS MORE INTO BALLET AND GYMNASTICS AND CHEERLEADER..

BRAD WAS THE ONLY CHILD, BUT WAS VERY POPULAR AT HIS ELEMETARY SCHOOL..

BRAD WAS SMALL FOR HIS AGE, BROWN HAIR AND BROWN EYES..

WHEN BRAD AND MARIA PLAYED TOGETHER THEY BOTH STOOD OUT, WITH BRAD BEING BROWN HAIR AND MARIA HAVING DARK BROWN HAIR AND BROWNEYES...

IN 1989, BRAD'S FATHER GOT WORD THAT THE FACTORY WHERE HE WORKED " A CAR PARTS FACTORY " WAS BEING MOVED TO THE WEST COAST SOMEWHERE IN THE MIDDLE OF CALIFORNIA WITHIN THE YEAR.

BRAD'S DAD TOLD HIS WIFE AND LITTLE BRAD WE HAVE TO MOVE BY THE END OF THE YEAR TO RELOCATE.. BRAD'S FIRST RESPONSE WAS " BUT WHAT ABOUT MY FRIENDS AND MARIA, CAN SHE COME WITH US? FATHERS RESPONSE WAS " NO I'M SORRY SON, BUT WE CAN VISIT AND YOU WILL MAKE NEW FRIENDS...
BRAD LOOKS SAD HANGS HIS HEAD DOWN AND SAY'S " OK "

THE FAMILIES CONTINUED THERE HABITS OF GETTING TOGETHER AND SPENDING AS MUCH TIME IN THE TOWN AND FAMILY, FRIENDS AS THEY CAN..

THE YEAR ROLLED ON TO A DAY IN AUGUST, IT WAS THE LAST JUDO CLASS THAT BRAD AND MARIA WOULD BE IN TOGETHER, THEY ARE 9 YEARS OLD, AT THE END OF THE CLASS BRAD WALKS OVER TO MARIA AND BOTH HAVE THEIR JUDO GI'S ON, BRAD TELLS HER " I WILL MISS YOU MARIA ' MARIA RESPONDS " I WILL MISS YOU TOO BRAD " I HAVE SOMETHING FOR YOU TO REMBER ME BY " HERE IS MY FAVORITE STUFFED DOG I SLEEP WITH   PATCHES .. EVERYTIME YOU SEE HIM YOU CAN THINK OF ME"
THEY BOTH HUGGED.. THE PARENTS WERE ALL READY TO LEAVE AS THE CLASS WAS OVER... A FEW DAYS LATER BRADS PARENTS WAS DONE PACKING AND LOADED UP TO LEAVE TO THE STATE OF CALIFORNIA. AFTER SAYING GOODBYES TO FAMILY AND FRIENDS THEY VENTURED OFF..

A WEEK WENT BY THEY FINALLY MOVED INTO THERE HOME IN CALIFORNIA AND GOT SETTLED IN, ENROLLED LITTLE BRAD INTO SCHOOL..

WEEKS AND MONTHS LATER THEY WERE GETTING USED TO THE BIG CITY LIFESTYLE..
BRAD'S PARENTS FOUND A JUDO SCHOOL IN CALIFORNIA, WAS THE BEST IN THE STATE,

OLYMPIANS WERE TRAINED THERE.. BRAD JOINED AND AUTOMATICALLY STILL LOVED THE JUDO, HE ALSO BECAME A BLACK BELT. HE ALSO FOUND THE LOVE OF WRESTLING IN SCHOOL, FOOTBALL... YEARS WENT BY, BRAD WAS A STAND OUT IN JR. HIGH AND HIGH SCHOOL, HONOR SOCIETY, WAS HOMECOMING KING….HE IS EIGHTEEN.

MEANWHILE IN THE MIDWEST, BACK IN THE SMALL TOWN OF OHIO, MARIA WAS AN ORDINARY KID, SHE WAS ALSO ON HONOR SOCIETY AND PLAYED SOCCER AND WAS STILL TAKING JUDO, SHE ACTUALLY WAS AN ASSISTANT COACH TO MR. BROWNS CLASSES, SHE AS WELL BECAME A BLACK BELT.. SHE IS ALSO EIGHTEEN AND A SENIOR.

HER LOVE FOR DOGS, BROUGHT HER TO VOLUNTEER TO A LOCAL DOG SHELTER ON A WEEKLY BASIS…

MONTHS WENT BY, SHE GRADUATED, WENT TO A COMMUNITY COLLEGE NOT FAR AWAY FROM HARRISONBURG, SHE GOT HER NURSING DEGREE AND WORKED AT THE SAME HOSPITAL HER AND BRAD WAS BORN IN… SHE MOVED ABOUT 5 MILES FROM HER PARENTS IN A SMALL WHITE HOUSE…

DATING, WELL SHE DATED ONLY 4 GUYS FROM THE TIME IN JR. HIGH TILL GRADUATION, NOTHING TOO SERIOUS…

HER OLDER SISTER WOULD ALWAYS TEASE HER NOW AND THEN SAYING " WHEN YOU GOING TO FIND MR. RIGHT " MARIA'S REPLIES WERE ALWAYS SOMETHING LIKE " MAYBE SOMEDAY "   HER FAMILY AND SHE ALL KNOW'S SHE HAS A BUSY LIFESTYLE, WORKING 12 HOUR SHIFTS, THEN TEACHING JUDO AND VOLUNTEER AT THE DOG SHELTER..

BACK IN CALIFORNIA, BRAD IS LIVING A GREAT LIFE, HE ENROLLED IN A LOCAL UNIVERSITY COLLEGE. WHERE HE HAD A WRESTLING SHCOLARSHIP.

HE GOT A JOB (PART TIME) WHILE IN COLLEGE, AT HIS FATHERS WORKPLACE, WHERE THEY MADE CAR PARTS… HE WAS DOING REALLY WELL FOR HIMSELF, HE AND HIS PARENTS WERE VERY HAPPY FOR HIM AND THEIR LIVES…

BRAD WAS SO INTO SPORTS, ABOUT EVERY SPORT ESCPECIALLY FOOTBALL..

MEANWHILE BACK IN OHIO, MARIA GOT A PROMOTION IN HER NURSING FIELD AND WAS NAMED NURSE OF THE YEAR AT THE HOSPITAL WHERE SHE WORKED..

HER FAMILY ARE FRIENDS HAD HER A SURPRISE PARTY TO CALABARATE HER ACCOMPLISHMENTS..

THEY RENTED A LOCAL HALL IN TOWN, WHERE IT NORMALLY HELD FOR MAINLY WEDDINGS…

THEY ALL HAD A BALL, DANCING, DJ'S, CAKE THEY HAD IT ALL, PACKED HOUSE WITH MOST OF THE STAFF THAT WORKED WITH HER AND THEN, JUST IMAGINE HER FAMILY AND FRIENDS….

SHE LOVED KIDS AND REALLY LIKES SPENDING TIME WITH HER NEPHEW AND NIECES.

MONDAY ROLLS AROUND, AND MARIA IS BACK TO THE GRIND OF HER 12HR. SHIFT..
BUT SHE LOVES WHAT SHE DOES. MARIA WAS LAID BACK AND NOT A BIG PARTIER, BUT

GOES OUT WITH THE GIRLS ON OCCASIONS..

BRAD'S ENGAGES IN A CAREER

SO BRAD GRADUATED FROM COLLEGE RECEIVING HIS DEGREE AND BECAME AN
ATTORNEY.
HE CONTINUED TO WORK AT HIS FATHERS WORKPLACE WHERE HIS FATHER WAS THE
VICE PRESIDENT OF THE COMPANY. HE WORKED FULL TIME NOW AND THEN TAUGHT
JUDO AND WRESTLING AT THE LOCAL JUDO ACADEMY, BUT NOW IT HAS GROWN INTO A
MMA TYPE GYM WHICH ADDED A CAGE ETC… SOON AFTER HIS DEGREE BRAD QUITS HIS
JOB AND STARTS WORKING FOR A GROUP OF ATTORNEY'S THEN EVENTUALLY GOES
WORKING FOR HIMSELF AND HAS HIS OWN OFFICE AND BECOMES SUCCESSFUL IN THE
LAW BUSINESS…

 MARIA DATES:

MARIA'S FRIEND AT WORK SAY'S TO HER " I THINK I KNOW A GUY WHO WOULD BE
PERFECT FOR YOU" MARIA'S REPLY IS " OK YEAH SURE" HER CO-WORKING REBECCA
REALLY WANTED TO FIX HER UP… SO MARIA DECIDED TO GIVE IT A TRY.. MARIA IS
GORGEOUS THINK, SHE IS HALF S AND HALF HISPANIC FROM HER MOTHERS SIDE OF
FAMILY, DARK BROWN EYE, LONG WAVY BLACK HAIR, CARMEL BROWN SKIN TONE,
ATHLETIC BUILD…..

MARIA AND THE DATE WENT WELL THAT NIGHT, THEY HAD A NICE DINNER AND A
MOVIE..
 THE GUY WAS A NICE GUY, NAMED MICHAEL FROM A TOWN CALLED FLORENCE
INDIANA, HE BEING A COUPLE YEARS OLDER THAN MARIA MADE IT COMPATIBLE. SHE
WAS 27 HE WAS 29, HAD A GOOD JOB, CAR, ETC.. THE DATED FOR 5 MONTHS,
EVERYTHING WAS GOOD.. THEN SLOWLY IT ENDED AFTER TIME. MARIA'S SCHEDULE
MADE IT IMPOSSIBLE FOR THEM TO DATE, SHE SOMETIMES WOULD WORK MORE THAN 12
HOURS AND THEN HER VOLUNTEER WORK WAS JUST TOO MUCH FOR MICHAEL, THE
BOTH DECIDED ON GOOD TERMS TO END THEIR RELATIONSHIP AND BECOME FRIENDS.
THEY DID JUST THAT…

BUT NOW MARIA AT HER AGE SHE ALWAYS WANTED TO BE MARRIED BY THE TIME SHE
WAS 30.. BUT SHE NEW IT DIDN'T SEEM POSSIBLE AS OF NOW..

BRAD IS AT WORK IN HIS OFFICE, HIS OFFICE PHONE RINGS, HIS RECEPTIONISH PAGES
HIM AND SAY'S " BRAD, YOUR MOTHER IS ON LINE 1 " BRAD SAY'S " PATCH HER
THROUGH RACHEL " BRAD ANSWERS " HELLO MOM " MRS. COLLINS REPLIES " HI DEAR "
DO YOU HAVE TIME THIS AFTERNOON TO HELP ME AND YOUR FATHER PUT UP
CHRISTMAS DECORATIONS ? BRAD REPLIES " MOM I HAVE TO GO OVER SOME
PAPERWORK FOR A CLIENT " MRS. COLLINS REPLIES " WELL WE REALLY WISH YOU
COULD COME OVER AND HELP, MOST OF OUR NEIGHBORS ALREADY GOT THEIR
DECORATIONS UP " BRAD'S THINKING, THEN HIS RECEPTIONIST WALKS IN WHILE HE IS
ON THE PHONE, SHE QUIETLY BEND OVER TO LAY A FOLDER OF PAPERS ON HIS DESK,
SHE OVERHEARD SOME OF THE CONVERSATION OF BRAD AND HIS MOTHER, SHE SMILES
AT HIM AND WHISPERS " BRAD, SHE IS YOUR MOTHER " WITH A SMILE " BRAD KIND OF A
FROWN SAY'S " OK MOM I WILL BE OVER AROUND FOURISH " MRS. COLLINS: " THANK
YOU, ME AND YOUR FATHER WILL SEE YOU SOON, BYE BYE..BRAD: BY MOM….
BRAD LOOKS AND HIS RECEPTIONIST AND TAKES A DEEP BREATH, RACHEL SAY'S "
YOU'RE A GOOD SON BRAD, WITH A GRIN AS SHE WALKS OUT.. BRAD SIT'S A MINUTE

JUMPS UP AND TALKS TO HIMSELF " TIME FOR LUNCH "

MARIA PUTTING UP HER DECORATIONS:

MARIA IS JUST FINISHING UP HER TREE, SHE LOOKS AT THE CLOCK AND REALIZES SHE
HAS GOT TO GET READY TO GO TO WORK.. SHE CHANGES INTO HER WORK CLOTHES
GETS IN HER VEHICLE AND LEAVES…AS SHE IS DRIVING ON HER WAY HER VEHICLE
STARTS TO BE ACTING UP LIKE IT'S LOSING POWER SHE LOOKS DOWN, " OH GREAT " SHE
NOTICES HER FUEL GAUGE READ'S " E " SHE KNOW'S SHE IS OUT OF GAS, SHE PULLS OFF
THE SIDE OF A RUAL ROAD AND PUTS THE VEHICLE IN PARK, SHE ATTEMPTS TO PULL
OUR HER CELL PHONE LOOKS AT THE PHONE AND THE PHONE IS DEAD.. MARIA " WHY
ME " ABOUT THAT TIME A GUY PULLS UP BESIDE HER WHICH HAPPENS TO BE A LOCAL
THAT IS A FRIEND, HE SHOUTS " HAVING TROUBLE WITH THE CAR AGAIN " MARIA
REPLEIS " HI CHARLEY, I'M OUT OF GAS " CHARLEY REPLIES " YOU KNOW THEY DON'T
RUN WITHOUT GAS , AS HE LAUGHED.. MARIA: I KNOW CHARLEY.. CHARLEY: COME ON
I'LL GIVE YOU A RIDE, WHERE WAS YOU HEADED TO? MARIA: WORK.. CHARLIE: JUMP
IN.. MARIA GET'S IN THE PASSENGER SIDE OF CHARLEY'S VEHICLE… CHARLEY: I WILL
GO GET A CAN OF GAS AT HOME AND PUT SOME GAS IN IT FOR YOU AND DROP IT OFF AT
YOUR WORK… MARIA: OH THANK YOU SO MUCH CHARLEY YOU ARE A LIFESAVER..
CHARLEY: WELL YOUR WELCOME… MARIA: SEE THAT'S WHY I LOVE THIS TOWN.. THEY
BOTH LAUGHED….

BRAD GOES TO PARENTS

BRAD PULLS IN HIS PARENTS DRIVEWAY, HE GETS OUT OF HIS CAR, WALKS TO THE
DOOR, RINGS THE BELL, MOM GREETS HIM, I BEEN WAITING FOR YOU… BRAD WALKS IN,
SHE POINTS TO THE ATTIC, HE GOES TO THE ATTIC STARTS LOOKING AT BOXES THAT
SAY XMAS ON THE BOXES… THEN AS HE PULLS OUT A BOX HE SEE'S ONE BOX BEHIND IT
PARTIALLY HIDDEN, THAT READS " HARRISONBURGH " HE GENTLY PULLS THE BOX
OUT, THEN HE LOOKS WITH A SOLID LOOK ON HIS FACE… HE WALKS IN THE KITCHEN
PUTS THE BOX ON THE TABLE OPENS THE BOX, HE SEE'S PICTURES OF HIM AND MARIA
AS KIDS HE SMILES AS HE LOOKS AT THEM, THEN AT THE BOTTOM HE SEE'S A STUFFED
ANIMAL IT'S " PATCHES " THE STUFFED ANIMAL DOG THAT MARIA GAVE HIM, HE
SMILES AND HE WALKS INTO A ROOM AND SEE'S HIS MOM HE ASKS HER " MOM, YOU
REMEMBER THE JOHNSON FAMILY BACK IN HARRISVILLE? MRS. COLLINS: WHY YES
SUCH A WONDERFUL FAMILY, OH YOU AND MARIA WERE INSEPARABLE, YOU TWO
WOULD PLAY AND GO EVERYWHERE TOGETHER, I REALLY HOPE THEY ARE ALL DOING
WELL… BRAD: " I WOULD LIKE TO SEE HOW MARIA AND HER FAMILY IS DOING " MRS.
COLLINS: WELL DEAR, TRY TO FIND OUT " BRAD: I WILL LOOK HER UP ONE WAY OR THE
OTHER…. MRS. COLLINS: SHE WOULD BE HAPPY TO HEAR FROM YOU I'M SURE…BRAD
SMILES….

HE IS HOME DIGGING UP INFO AND TRYING TO FIND HER NAME AND INFORMATION, HE'S
HAVING A TIME FINDING IT. SO HE LEANS BACK IN HIS CHAIR PUTS HIS HANDS ON HIS
HEAD IN FRUSTRATION. TURNS THE COMPUTER OFF FOR THE NIGHT, HE IS OFF TO BED…

NEXT MORNING HE IS IN HIS OFFICE, HE CALLS IN HIS RECEPTIONIST RACHEL IN, SHE
WALKS IN… BRAD: MORNING RACHEAL, WOULD YOU DO ME A FAVOR? RACHEL : I'LL
DO MY BEST…. BRAD: CAN YOU BOOK ME ON A FLIGHT TO HARRISVILLE? I THINK I
MIGHT GO THEIR A COUPLE DAYS OVER THE HOLIDAY BREAK… RACHEL: OK, ANY

REASON WHY YOU WANT TO GO BACK THERE? BRAD: TO SEE OLD FRIENDS… RACHEL: GOTCHA, I WILL GET ON IT… BRAD: THANK YOU…

MARIA IS COOKING DINNER FOR A FRIEND THAT'S COMING OVER

MARIA IS JUST FINISHING UP BAKING CHICKEN AND GETTING THE POTATO'S READY FOR HER FRIEND BECKY THAT IS SOON TO ARRIVE…
DOOR BELL RINGS….. MARIA OPENS THE DOOR " HELLO MY BESTIE " BECKY AND MARIA HUG… BECKY- MMM SMELLS GOOD, I'M HUNGRY.. MARIA - WELL LETS EAT…

AS THE TWO ARE EATING THEY ARE TALKING ABOUT WORK AND A CONCERT THEY ARE SOON TO ATTEND IN THE SPRING… THEN BECKY MENTIONS " SO WE NEED TO HAVE A GIRLS NIGHT OUT AND GO DANCING AND FIND YOU A GUY "   MARIA - I'M NOT TRYING TO FIND A GUY, LET HIM FIND ME, AS SHE LAUGHS…. BECKY- I KNOW MAYBE SOON HE WILL JUST SHOW UP… MARIA- YEAH RIGHT, THE WAY MY LUCK IS WITH MEN I WOULDN'T KNOW IT IF HE WAS STANDING IN FRONT OF ME…. SO THE TWO FINISH THERE'RE DINNER AND BECKY GIVES RACHEAL A HUG, THEN HEADS FOR THE DOOR… MARIA IS TIRED SO SHE CHANGES INTO HER BED CLOTHES, BRUSHES HER TEETH THEN HIT'S THE BED FOR THE NIGHT…..

BRAD GOES TO WORK

BRAD ARRIVES IN HIS OFFICE TURNS HIS LIGHT ON SITS DOWN, THEN RACHEL WALKS IN… RACHEAL- GOOD MORNING BRAD, HEY I BOOKED YOU ON A FLIGHT TOO HARRISONVILLE…. BRAD- YOU DID? YOU'RE THE BEST RACHEL, I ALSO GOT YOU A HOTEL IN BRIGHTVILLE INDIANA JUST UP THE HILL FROM HARRISONBURG OHIO.. BRAD- YES BRIGHTVILLE INDIANA, I SPENT A LOT OF TIME THERE IN MY YOUTH, I MISS IT THERE TOO…. RACHEL- WELL I GUESS YOU ARE GOING TO GO THEN… BRAD-YES, THANK YOU FOR GETTING ME BOOKED AND HANDLING THE DETAILS ON MY MINI GETWAY…. RACHEL- YOU BET…….

BRAD STARTS HIS DAY AT WORK WITH PICKING UP THE PHONE AND MAKING CALLS TO HIS CLIENTS AND CHECKING EMAILS AS WELL….

CHRISTMAS IS COMING SOON, SO BRAD IS GOING TO BE OFF WORK FOR AWHILE SO HE HAS TIME TO GO BACK TO HARRISONBURG…

AS THE DAY ENDS, HE DRIVES STRAIGHT HOME TO START PACKING AND GETTING THINGS READY FOR THE TRIP….. HE IS FINALLY DONE PACKING AND EXHAUSTED SO SHOWER TIME AND BED…….

NEXT MORNING,

BRAD GETS UP EATS BREAKFAST, AFTER THE MEAL HE GETS DRESSED AND OFF TO THE AIRPORT….

MEANWHILE IN HARRISONBURG. MARIA IS GETTING READY TO GO SHOPPING FOR A WEDDING SHE WAS INVITED TOO, ONE OF HER GOOD FRIENDS (JENNIFER) IS GETTING MARRIED IN A TOWN NORTHEAST OF HARRISONBURG,(CLEVENSVILLE) WHICH IS ABOUT A 3 HOUR DRIVE AWAY… MARIA MET UP WITH A COUPLE FRIENDS TO LUNCH AND THEN OFF TO THE SHOPPING, THE ARE ALL SHOPPING FOR GIFTS AND SOME LAST MINUTE CLOTHING ITEMS… THE TWO FRIENDS THAT ARE JOINING MARIA TODAY IS BECKY AND ANGIE, THE GO TO THE SMALL COFFEE SHOP TO DRINK COFFEE AND EAT A LITTLE, ANGIE SAY'S " HEY YOU TWO READY TO HIT THE STORES? MARIA AND BECKY BOTH REPLY IN A MODERATE TONE " YES WE ARE "   SO THEY ALL THREE LEFT THE COFFEE SHOP AND JUMPED INTO MARIA'S JEEP AND OFF THEY GO TO THE SHOPPING STORES..

BRAD'S ARRIVAL TO THE AIRPORT..

BRAD I GETTING HIS TICKET TO TRAVEL TO HARRISONBURG, HE GET HIS TICKET GOES THROUGH THE GATE AND OFF ONTO THE JET….. HE SETS IN HIS SEAT AFTER PUTTING A FEW THINGS OUT LIKE HIS " PHONE, MAGAZINE, HEADPHONES " .. NEXT TO HIM IS AN ELDERLY LADY SHE SAY'S " HI MY NAME IS MARIA " BRAD REPLIES " I'M BRAD AND ONE OF MY BEST FRIEND'S I AM HEADING TO SEE HOPEFULLY I CAN FIND HER, HER NAME IS MARIA ALSO " AS HE CHUCKLED A LITTLE…. BRAD GETS SITUATED IN THE SEAT AND SMILES THINKING IN HIS HEAD (THIS IS MEANT FOR ME TO FIND HER)…
THE LADY SAID " FIRST TIME FLYING? " BRAD REPLIES " NO MA'AM, I HAVE BEEN ON MANY FLIGHTS MAINLY FOR BUSINESS "
THE LADY AND CHILD SITTING IN FRONT OF BRAD OVER HEARING THE CONVERSATION, SAYING " I HATE TO INTERRUPT YOUR CONVERSATION BUT THIS IS NOT MY FIRST RODEO EITHER, I FLY SEVERAL TIMES A YEAR, BY THE WAY MY DAUGHTER SITTING HERE HER NAME IS MARIA ANN IS HER FIRST AND MIDDLE NAME, (LAUGHING)
BRAD (WOW SO COOL, THE OLD FRIEND I AM VISITING HER NAME IS MARIA AND THIS LADY NEXT TO ME IS NAME IS MARIA… ALL FOUR OF THEM LAUGH INCLUDING THE CHILD… AS THE PLANE IS READY FOR TAKE OFF THEY ALL START TO SMILE AND GET TO KNOW EACH OTHER AND TALK AS THE JET IS GEARING FOR TAKE OFF….

BACK IN HARRISBURG OHIO, MARIA AND FRIENDS ARE SHOPPING AISLE AFTER AISLE
WITH ALL THE CLOTHES AND AT THE SAME TIME CHRISTMAS ITEMS ON DISPLAY AT THE
SAME TIME IS PUTTING THE GIRLS IN A CHRISTMAS MOOD… BECKY FINDS A NICE DRESS
(HEY YOU LIKE THIS DRESS?) MARIA REPLIES (OH YES THAT LOOKS SO GOOD BECKY)
ANGIE JUMPS IN AND OPENS HER MOUTH (YES I AGREE IT LOOKS NICE)
SO BECKY WALKS INTO THE DRESSING ROOM TO TRY THE DRESS ON.. AS SHE IS
CHANGING, MARIA AND ANGIE ARE STAYING CLOSE TO THE DRESSING ROOM WAITING
ON BECKY…
BECKY WALKS OUT OF DRESSING ROOM… MARIA AND ANGIE GOT QUIET….. THEN THE
GIRLS ARE LOOKING HAPPY TELLING ANGIE IT LOOKS SO GOOD ON HER….. SO BECKY
DECIDES TO BUY THE DRESS AND A FEW MINOR ADJUSTMENTS FOR FITTING FROM THE
CLERK…. THEN MARIA LOOKS AT SOME DRESSES…. ANGIE (WELL BECKY'S GOT HER
DRESS I ALREADY GOT MINE LAST WEEK, SO NOW IT'S YOUR TURN MARIA)..
MARIA STARTS TO LOOK AROUND SHE FINDS ONE THAT PEAKS HER INTEREST..
MARIA (I THINK I WILL TRY THIS ONE ON) SHE WALKS IN TO THE DRESSING ROOM, IT
FITS PERFECT SHE WALKS OUT….
BECKY (OH MY)   ANGIE (WOW WOW WOW)   ANGIE (MARIA YOU LOOK GORGEOUS)
ANGIE (YOU WILL MAKE A GREAT BRIDE SOMEDAY MARIA)
MARIA (YOU THING SO?)
BECKY AND ANGIE BOTH SHAKE THEY'RE HEAD YES)
SO THE GIRLS PURCHASE THE DRESSES AND OTHER GIFTS AT THE COUNTER…
THEY WALK OUT TO THE CAR AND ARE ALMOST READY FOR THEM TO GO THE WEDDING.
SO THEY GO HOME TO EACH OF THEY'RE HOUSES AND ANGIE IS PICKING MARIA AND
BECKY UP TO DRIVE TO THE WEDDING….. AND HOUR PASSES AND ANGIE IS ON HER WAY
TO PICK UP BECKY FIRST THEN MARIA….

MEANWHILE BRAD'S PLANE IS STILL IN THE AIR, STILL HAVE A COUPLE HOURS YET
BEFORE DESTINATION….

FINALLY THE JET LANDS, BRAD WALKS OFF PLANE AND INTO THE AIRPORT, HE CHECK'S
OUT HIS LUGGAGE AND WALKS OUT TO GET INTO HIS RENT A CAR WHICH IS A BLACK
FULL SIZE SUV….. HE GETS IN AND GETS SITUATED AND DRIVES TO HIS HOTEL, HE
CHECK'S IN TO THE HOTEL UNPACKS HIS BELONGINGS AND JUMPS BACK IN TO HIS SUV
TO GO LOOK AROUND THE TOWN HE LEFT SO MANY YEARS AGO…. HE DRIVES PAST
ELEMENTARY SCHOOL, HE NOTICES THAT THE TOWN IS NOW ACTUALLY A CITY NOW, HE
COMES UPON THE RESTAURANTS THAT HE REMEMBERED HIS PARENTS WOULD ALWAYS
GO TO   PARTON'S FAMILY DINER   BRAD PULLS IN A PARKING SPOT, WALKS IN HE SEES
A FEW COUPLES EATING IN THE BOOTHS HE SETS DOWN, A WAITRESS WALKS UP
(HELLO WELCOME TO PARTON'S FAMILY DINER MY NAME IS AMBER I WILL BE
ASSISTING YOU TODAY, HERE'S THE SPECIALS FOR TODAY, I WILL GIVE YOU A MINUTE,
WHAT TO DRINK?) BRAD REPLIES (A COLA AND I THINK I WILL HAVE A CHEESE BURGER
PLAIN AND AN ORDER OF FRIES AND THAT SHOULD BE ALL) AMBER THE WAITRESS (OK
WILL HAVE THAT OUT FOR YOU IN A BIT) BRAD (THANK YOU)..

ABOUT 10 MINUTES PASSES BY, THE WAITRESS BRINGS HIS FOOD AND TO HIS TABLE,
ALREADY HAS HIS COLA HALF GONE.. BRAD (CAN I HAVE A REFILL) AMBER THE
WAITRESS (OF COURSE)   BRAD THEN LOOKS AT THE WAITER AND ASK HER …
BRAD (EXCUSE ME DO YOU KNOW OR HEARD OF MARIA JOHNSON?) WAITER (WHY YES,
SHE LIVE OUT OFF OF CAROLINA STREET) BRAD (I AM TRYING TO REACH HER)
WAITER (WELL HUN SHE WAS JUST IN HERE A FEW DAY'S AGO, ARE YOU A FRIEND OF
HERS?)

BRAD (YES AND OLD OLD FRIEND)
WAITER (CHUCKLES)
BRAD FINISHES THE MEAL AND LEAVES A TIP
WAITER (THANK YOU DARLING, COME AND SEE US AGAIN, AND HOPE YOU FIND MARIA)
BRAD (THANK YOU AND HAPPY HOLIDAY'S)

BRAD NOTICES THAT IT'S COLDER HERE THAN IN SUNNY CALIFORNIA, BUT IT'S GETTING
DUSK SOON SO HE DECIDES TO LOOK UP MARIA'S ADDRESS ON THE INTERNET FROM HIS
PHONE AS HE SITS IN HIS CAR… THE NAME AND ADDRESS POPS UP AND HE KNOWS
THAT'S HER FOR SURE WHEN HE SEES CAROLINA STREET…. SO HE PROCEEDS TO DRIVE,
6 MINUTES PASS HE PULLS INTO HER DRIVE WAY, HE OPENS THE DOOR OF HIS CAR, AND
GETS OUT AND WALKS UP TO THE DOOR, HE RINGS THE DOOR BELL AND KNOCKS, HE
WAIT'S A MINUTE OR SO RINGS DOOR BELL AND KNOCKS AGAIN, NO ANSWER… SO HE
GETS BACK INTO HIS SUV AND DRIVES OFF… HE STOPS INTO A JOHN'S GAS AND
GROCERY WHICH HE KNEW WAS HERE BEFORE HE LEFT TO CALIFORNIA.. HE WALKS IN
AND AN OLDER GENTLEMAN BEHIND THE COUNTER SAYS (HELLO)
BRAD (HELLO, CAN YOU HELP ME WITH SOMETHING?) SURE SAID THE CLERK..
BRAD (I AM LOOKING FOR MARIA JOHNSON, A FRIEND, I FOUND HER ADDRESS AND NO
ONE WAS HOME, DO YOU KNOW HERE?) THE CLERK (WHY YES SIR I DO, HER PARENTS
LIVE ON BROADWAY AVENUE) THE CLERK WRITES DOWN THE ADDRESS OF THE
JOHNSONS…
BRAD (OH THANK YOU SIR, BY THE WAY I USED TO COME HERE AS A CHILD, DO THE
ORIGINAL OWNERS STILL HERE ?) THE CLERK (WELL YES, BUT I AM JOHN'S SON, SO WE
KINDA RUN IT SINCE MY FATHER RETIRED)
BRAD (OH THAT IS GOOD, AND THANK YOU FOR THE INFORMATION MY FRIEND)
THE CLERK (NO PROBLEM BUDDY YOU HAVE A GOOD ONE)
BRAD WAVES AND WALKS OUT AND STOPS AND THINKING HOW FRIENDLY THIS TOWN
STILL IS AS HE LEFT AS A CHILD….

BRAD LOOKS AT THE ADDRESS AND TAKES OFF TO DRIVE, 4 MINUTES AND HE IS IN THE
DRIVEWAY… HE GETS OUT OF VEHICLE AND WALKS UP AND RINGS DOOR BELL
SOMEONE LOOKS OUT, A LADY OPENS THE DOOR (HELLO)
BRAD (HI MA'AM I DON'T KNOW AND DOUBT YOU REMEMBER ME BUT FIRST ARE YOU
MRS. JOHNSON?)
THE LADY LOOKS AT HIM AND SAYS (YES I AM, MY NAME IS SUE)
BRAD (I WILL TELL YOU ABOUT ME, I USED TO LIVE NEAR YOU WHEN I WAS A KID AND
USED TO PLAY WITH YOU DAUGHTER MARIA AND YOU WERE GOOD FRIENDS WITH MY
PARENTS THE COLLINS)
SUE (OH OH OH BRAD?)
BRAD (YES)
SUE HUGS HIM AND SAYING (YOU HAVE GROWN UP SO MUCH, YOUR SUCH A HANDSOME
YOUNG MAN , (NOTE: BRAD IS 6'2 WIDE SHOULDERS SHORT BROWN HAIR BLUE EYES
GOOD BUILD AND GOOD LOOKS)…HOW YOU BEEN AND WHAT BRINGS YOU BACK TO
HARRISONBURG?)
BRAD (I ACTUALLY WANTED TO VISIT MARIA)
SUE (WELL SHE IS GONE UNTIL SUNDAY, SHE IS AT FRIENDS WEDDING)
BRAD (OH THAT'S NICE SHE WILL HAVE FUN I'M SURE)
SUE (WANT ME TO GIVE HER YOUR NUMBER SO SHE CAN CONTACT YOU?)
BRAD (YES PLEASE DO)
BRAD GIVES MARIA'S MOTHER HIS NUMBER AND GIVES HER A HUG AND DRIVES BACK
TO THE HOTEL WITH A SMILE ON HIS FACE….

SUE CALLS MARIA, MARIA SEE'S HER CELL PHONE CALLER ID AND IT SAY'S " MOM "
MARIA QUICKLY TELLS THE GIRLS AND EVERYONE AROUND (EXCUSE ME I HAVE TO
TAKE THIS CALL)   SHE FINDS A QUIET PLACE NEAR A DINING ROOM AND HALL.. MARIA

(HI MOM)   SUE (HI DEAR, I HATE TO INTERRUPT YOUR GOOD TIME, BUT A HANDSOME YOUNG MAN STOPPED BY TO SEE YOU)   MARIA (WHO MOM?)
SUE (DO YOU REMEMBER BRAD COLLINS?) MARIA THINK'S A FEW SECONDS AND SHE KIND OF REMEMBERS.. MARIA (ANY RELATIONS TO THE COLLINS WE WAS NEIGHBORS TOO, YEAR BACK?)
SUE (YES IT IS STEVE AND SARA'S SON BRAD, THE BOY YOU USED TO PLAY WITH AND TAKE JUDO LESSONS WITH)
MARIA (OH OK YES, HOW IS HE?)
SUE (HE IS DOING WELL DEAR, HE IS SUCH A HANDSOME YOUNG MAN HE'S 6'2 CLEAN CUT BLUE EYES AND KIND AS CAN BE)
MARIA (DID YOU LEAVE?)
SUE (YES HE IS LEAVING I BELIEVE BACK HOME SOON, BUT HE LEFT HIS NUMBER)
MARIA (OK KEEP IT AND I WILL GET IT WHEN I GET BACK IN TOWN)
SUE (OK DEAR, STAY SAFE HAVE A GOOD TIME, I LOVE YOU BYE)
MARIA (I LOVE YOU TO MOM, BYE NOW)

BRAD PULLS IN TO THE HOTEL PARKING LOT, GETS OUT OF THE SUV AND WALKS INTO THE HOTEL ROOM, SO HE CHANGES CLOTHES AND GRABS A SNACK AND SODA LAYS ON BED AND WATCHES TV, TILL HE GETS A LITTLE TIRED, FINALLY AN HOUR OR SO PASSES BY HE GOES TO THE BATHROOM TO BRUSH HIS TEETH THEN TURNS THE LIGHT OUT AND GOES TO SLEEP……

NEXT MORNING BRAD WAKES UP AND IS TIME TO GET READY TO GO BACK HOME, HE GETS DRESSED AND EATS A BOWL OF OATMEAL AND BANANA AND IS OFF TO CATCH HIS FLIGHT…….

AT THE SAME TIME MARIA AND THE GIRLS ARE GETTING READY TO DRIVE BACK HOME FROM THE WEDDING AND RECEPTION

BRAD IS NOW BACK ON PLANE AND IS IN THE AIR ON THE WAY BACK TO CALIFORNIA. HOURS PASS THE PLANE LANDS HE IS NOW READY TO GO HOME AND UNPACK AND GET SITUATED BACK TO HIS BUSY NORMAL LIFE AGAIN….. HE FINALLY MAKES IT HOME UNPACKS, HE DECIDES TO GO VISIT HIS PARENTS..
HE ARRIVES AND HIS PARENTS ARE OUTSIDE HANGING UP CHRISTMAS ORNAMENTS, HE PULLS IN GETS OUT OF HIS VEHICLE BRAD (HI MOM) SARA (BRAD'S MOM) HI HONEY, DID YOU HAVE A GOOD TRIP? BRAD (YES I DID) SARA (DID YOU SEE ANY OF OUR OLD FRIENDS?) BRAD (YES I TALKED TO MARIA'S MOTHER ALSO) SARA (GREAT SWEETHEART)

BRAD - I THINK I WILL GET A HOLD OF MARIA VERY SOON, SHE WAS AWAY AT A FRIEND'S WEDDING ABOUT 2 HOURS AWAY FROM WHERE SHE LIVES….

SARA (BRAD'S MOM) - WELL GOOD, I LIKE TO SEE THAT FAMILY AGAIN AND GO BACK TO VISIT OUR OLD TOWN..

BRAD - YES MOTHER, IT HAS CHANGED SOME WITH NEW STORES AND MALLS, BUT THE PEOPLE ARE STILL THE MOST NICEST WELCOMING PEOPLE AROUND..

SARA (BRAD'S MOM) - WELL WE ALL BETTER PLAN A TRIP OUT THERE IN THE NEAR FUTURE.. DID YOU HAPPEN TO DRIVE BY OUR OLD HOUSE? BRAD - NO BUT NEXT TIME I

WILL FOR SURE..

SARA (BRAD'S MOM) - WILL YOU HELP WITH HANGING UP SOME OF THESE CHRISTMAS ORNAMENTS?
BRAD - SURE MOM…
SO BRAD STARTS TO HELP HIS PARENTS SORT THE ORNAMENTS OUT IN THE FRONT YARD…

MARIA THE GIRLS HAVE ARRIVED BACK THE TOWN AFTER A COUPLE HOURS ON THE ROAD.

MARIA DROPS OFF BOTH ANGIE AND BECKY, MARIA IS TIRED OF DRIVING AND HEADS TOWARDS HOME, SHE SAYS TO HERSELF SOFTLY " ALMOST HOME "

MARIA ARRIVES HOME ENTERS HER HOME TAKES OFF HER SHOES JUMPS ONTO THE COUCH AND FINDS THE REMOTE AND TURNS ON THE TV AND TAKES HER PHONE OUT…

MARIA CALLS HER MOM TO LET HER KNOW SHE MADE IT HOME AND WILL STOP OVER LATER TO GET HER MAIL THAT HER MOTHER HAS GOT FOR HER SINCE SHE LEFT FOR THE TRIP TO THE WEDDING…

AS MARIA IS HAVING A CONVERSATION OVER THE PHONE WITH HER MOM, MARIA ALMOST FORGETS TO ASK, MARIA - OH MOM CAN I HAVE THE NUMBER OF BRAD?
SUE (MARIA'S MOM) - WHY YES DEAR, LET ME GO TO THE KITCHEN TO GRAB IT WHERE I WROTE IT DOWN..
MARIA - SURE MOM I WILL WAIT…
SUE - OH MARIA I HOPE I DIDN'T ACCIDENTALLY THREW IT AWAY.
MARIA - MOM NO..
SUE - OH WAIT HERE IT IS.
MARIA - WHOA I THOUGH YOU LOST IT.
SUE - ME TOO.

SO SUE GIVES HER DAUGHTER THE NUMBER THAT BRAD LEFT HER.., THE EXCHANGE GOOD BYE'S AND BOTH HANG UP…

SO MARIA IS THINKING AND LOOKING AT THE NUMBER SHE HAS PUT INTO HER PHONE, SHE IS THINKING SHOULD I CALL OR TEXT, IT'S LIKE MARIA IS TRYING TO DECIDE IS THIS THE RIGHT TIME TO GET IN TOUCH WITH BRAD OR NOT…

SO MARIA DECIDES TO TEXT BRAD… TEXT - HELLO BRAD, THIS IS MARIA

BRAD IS OUT IN HIS PARENTS YARD STILL HELPING WITH THE ORNAMENTS, HIS PHONE IS LEFT IN HIS VEHICLE AND HE DOES NOT HEAR THE TEXTING TONE….

BRAD GOES BACK TO HIS VEHICLE TO GET ANOTHER LUGGAGE BAG AND SOME GOODIES THAT WAS IN THE BAG, HE SAW HIS PHONE AND PICKS IT UP AND LOOKS AT IT AND NOTICES IT HAS A MISSED TEXT, READS - HELLO BRAD, THIS IS MARIA

SO BRAD GOES INTO HIS PARENTS HOUSE AND DROPS OFF AND GIVES HIS MOM A CHRISTMAS ORNAMENT THAT HE PICKED UP IN HARRISVILLE, AND TELLS HER HE GOT

ALL THE DECORATIONS UP, AND IS HEADING HOME FOR THE NIGHT….

BRAD IS HOME AND RELAXING HE DECIDES TO TEXT THE NUMBER BACK IT READS "
HELLO THIS IS BRAD "   HE LAYS THE PHONE DOWN GOES TO THE FRIDGE TO GET A
DRINK OF WATER AS HE WALKS BACK HE SEE'S THAT THERE IS ANOTHER NEW TEXT "
HELLO HOW ARE YOU BRAD? THIS IS MARIA…
BRAD'S TEXT : MARIA I'M SO HAPPY YOU GOT IN TOUCH WITH ME, I WANT TO MEET UP
WITH YOU SOMETIME WHEN I COME BACK TO YOUR TOWN..
MARIA'S TEXT: SURE BRAD ANYTIME YOU COME BACK DOWN HERE, PLEASE CONTACT
ME AHEAD OF TIME SO I CAN MEET UP..
BRAD'S TEXT: I FOR SURE WILL, I CAN'T WAIT TO CATCH UP WITH YOU..
MARIA'S TEXT: IT WILL BE A TREAT FOR SURE
BRAD'S TEXT: SO I WILL GET A HOLD OF YOU SOON AND ASK YOU FOR DINNER WHEN I
COME TO TOWN..
MARIA'S TEXT: YOU GOT YOURSELF A DATE.. I WILL KEEP IN TOUCH, YOU HAVE A GREAT
NIGHT BRAD, I GOT TO GET UP EARLY FOR WORK.. GREAT TALKING TO YOU AGAIN..
BRAD'S TEXT: YOU TOO MARIA, GOOD NIGHT…

NEXT MORNING….
BRAD IS ON HIS WAY TO WORK, HE IS THINKING HE IS OFF FOR TWO WEEKS AFTER HIS
DOES SOME PAPERWORK AT THE OFFICE AND PICK UP FILES…..

HE DECIDES THAT HE IS GOING BACK TO HARRISONBURG OF HOPING TO SEE MARIA..

BRAD CALLS HIS PARENTS AND TELLS THEM THAT HE IS LEAVING BACK TO
HARRISONBURG IN A COUPLE DAYS AGAIN….

HIS PARENTS TELL HIM TO BE CAREFUL AND SAY HI TO ALL THE FRIENDS DOWN THERE..

BRAD IS GETTING EXCITED KNOWING HE WILL SEE MARIA AGAIN AFTER ALL…

BRAD LEAVES WORK, GOES HOME CALLS AND MAKES RESERVATIONS TO
HARRISONBURG ONCE AGAIN….

HE TEXT MARIA TELLING HER IS WILL BE IN HARRISONBURG IN TWO DAYS..

MARIA IS OFF FOR A WEEK IN A HALF HERSELF SO SHE TELLS HIM SHE WILL BE AROUND
WHEN HE ARRIVES….

NEXT MORNING..

BRAD IS ALREADY ON THE PLANE ABOUT TO TOUCHDOWN NEAR HARRISONBURG, HIM
AND MARIA HAS MADE ARRANGEMENTS TO MEET AT A LOCAL STEAKHOUSE….

HE GETS INTO HIS RENT-A-CAR, AND MAKES IT TO HI HOTEL… HE IS GETTING READY TO
GO MEET MARIA…

MEANWHILE, MARIA IS FRESHENING UP AND ON HER WAY TO THE RESTAURANT…

MARIA ARRIVES AND IS EARLY, SHE SETS DOWN WAITING AND SOMEWHAT NERVOUS..

10 MINUTES GOES BY, SHE KEEPS LOOKING AT EVERYONE COMING IN THE DOOR, TO SEE IF IT'S BRAD…. FINALLY THE DOOR OPENS, SHE LOOKS ACROSS THE ROOM AND SEE'S A HANDSOME MAN DRESSED NICE AND WELL GROOMED, SHE NOTICES HE IS LOOKING AROUND, SHE GETS NERVOUS, HE MAKES EYE CONTACT WITH MARIA, SHE SMILES AND HE SMILES SHE WAVES HER HAND, HE WALKS OVER…

BRAD WALK'S OVER AND MARIA STANDS UP TO GIVE EACH OTHER A HUG….

BRAD - HOW YOU BEEN?
MARIA- GOOD, AND HOW ARE YOU BRAD?
BRAD - GOOD.
BRAD - I AM GOING TO ORDER ME A STEAK, AND I'M BUYING, WHAT DO YOU WANT MARIA?
MARIA - I'LL TAKE THE SAME (THEY BOTH CHUCKLE)

THEY BOTH TALK AND CHAT THROUGH THE MEAL, AND DECIDE TO GO FOR A WALK DOWN ON THE MAIN STREET TO SEE ALL THE CHRISTMAS DECORATIONS AFTER THE DINNER…

BRAD TELLS MARIA THAT HE WILL DRIVE HER TO TOWN WHERE THE CHRISTMAS LIGHTS ARE AT… SHE JUMPS IN THE VEHICLE AND THEY DRIVE DOWN TO THE MAIN STREET WHERE IT'S TRADITION WHERE THE LIGHTS ARE FESTIVE…..

THEY TALK ABOUT THE TOWN HASN'T CHANGED MUCH SINCE HE LEFT TO MOVE ON THE WEST COAST MANY YEARS AGO, THEY BOTH EXIT THE VEHICLE AND WALK AND TALK WITH SMILES, THEY STOP BY A VENDOR SELLING SOME HOT CHOCOLATE, BRAD PURCHASES THE TWO STEAMING HOT CHOCOLATES FOR HIM AND MARIA…

MARIA IS GETTING COMFORTABLE BEING AROUND BRAD, SO AS THEY WALK THERE IS SOME SNOW ON THE GROUND SO MARIA ASK BRAD TO WALK DOWN THE STREET AND GO SLED RIDING, BRAD AGREES SO THEY MAKE THEY'RE WAY TO THE HILL WHERE ALL THE TOWNS PEOPLE, VISITORS AND CHILDREN ARE USING AND RENTING SLEDS..
MARIA RENTS TWO SLEDS SO HER AND BRAD RACE DOWN THE HILL LAUGHING AND YELLING…. BRAD GETS TO THE BOTTOM OF THE HILL AND FALLS OFF THE SIDE AND ROLLS ON THE GROUND, MARIA LAUGHS, BRAD LOOKS AT HER WITH A SMILE AND SAY'S " SO YOU THINK THAT'S FUNNY? "   BRAD PICKS UP A SNOW BALL AND THROWS IT AT MARIA… MARIA THROWS A SNOW BALL AT BRAD SOON IT BECOMES A SNOW BALL FIGHT WITH LAUGHS AND GIGGLES AS THE CHRISTMAS MUSIC IS PLAYING OVER THE PA AND SPEAKERS AT THE SITE, SOME START TO WATCH THE TWO ENGAGING IN A SNOW BALL FIGHT, SO OTHERS START TO JOIN IN AND NOW (MINUTES LATER) IT SEEMS TO BE MORE THAN 20 PEOPLE AND CHILDREN HAVING FUN EVERYONE FOR THEMSELVES, ALL HAVING SUCH A WONDERFUL TIME HERE….

BRAD AND MARIA FINALLY ARE FINISHED AND LOOK AT EACH OTHER SMILING THEN WALK TO A GIFT SHOP, THEY SPEND SOME TIME IN THERE LOOKING AT CHRISTMAS CRAFTS AND SOUVENIRS, MARIA PUTS A SANTA CLAUS HAT ON BRAD HE LOOKS IN THE MIRROR MAKES FACES……

AS THEY COME OUT OF THE SHOP THEY SEE PARENTS AND CHILDREN WAITING IN LINE TO GET A PICTURE WITH SANTA, BRAD SAY'S TO MARIA " LETS GET IN LINE "   MARIA - ARE YOU CRAZY? (LAUGHING) THEN GET IN LINE, ABOUT 4 MINUTES PAST THE BOTH COME WALKING UP TO SANTA, MARIA SETS ON SANTA'S KNEE, BRAD STANDS ON THE LEFT SIDE OF SANTA'S CHAIR AND THE LADY TAKING PICTURES FOR THE TOWNS PEOPLE AND HAVE PICTURES OF THE CHILDREN AND WHOM EVER GOES TO SANTA, THE LADY

TAKES A PICTURE OF BRAD AND MARIA WITH SANTA, THEY GET THE PICTURE AND TELL
THEM THANKS AND AS THEY WALK AWAY THEY BOTH ARE LOOKING AT THE PICTURE..

THEY BOTH SMILE AND KNOW IT TURNED OUT GREAT….

AS THEY WALK TO BRAD'S VEHICLE (BLACK SUV) THEY BOTH ENTER THE VEHICLE AS
BRAD STARTS TO DRIVE AWAY, MARIA ASK - SO YOU GOING BACK TO YOUR HOTEL ?
BRAD - YES IT IS GETTING LATE
MARIA - YOUR RIGHT IT IS, I GOT TO GET UP EARLY TO HELP MOM MAKE COME COOKIES
AND CAKES THEY CHRISTMAS USUAL TRADITION WE BAKE EVERY YEAR…

AS BRAD PULLS UP TO MARIA'S HOUSE TO DROP HER OFF, MARIA ASK BRAD - DO YOU
WANT TO COME IN FOR A BIT?
BRAD - SURE
AS BRAD WALK'S IN BEHIND MARIA, BRAD SAY'S " NICE PLACE "
MARIA - THANK YOU, IT'S NOT THE BIGGEST HOUSE BUT IT'S HOME..
BRAD - I REALLY MISS THIS TOWN

BRAD LOOKS AROUND AND NOTICES THE CHRISTMAS STAR IS CROOKED, HE TELLS
MARIA THAT THE STAR IS NOT ON STRAIGHT..

MARIA WALKS BACK INTO THE LIVING ROOM WHERE THE CHRISTMAS TREE IS AT.
MARIA - OH THE STAR IS CROOKED, I BETTER STRAIGHTEN IT UP
MARIA GOES AND GRABS THE STEP STOLL, SHE WALKS UP THE STEP AND STRETCHES
HER ARM UP.

BRAD IS STANDING ON THE LEFT SIDE OF HER AND STEP STOLL, AS MARIA STRAIGHTENS
THE STAR UP SHE LOOSES HER BALANCE AND FALLS TO THE LEFT, BRAD CATCHES HER
AND SHE FALLS INTO HIS ARMS THE SPIN AROUND AND HE LOSES HIS BALANCE ALSO
AND FALLS OVER THE ARM OF COUCH ONTO THE COUCH, HE LANDS ON HIS BACK AND
MARIA IS ON TOP THEY ARE LOOKING FACE TO FACE, THEY BOTH ARE SMILING, THEY'RE
FACES ARE INCHES AWAY FROM EACH OTHER… AS THEY BOTH WERE THINKING ABOUT
KISSING EACH OTHER, BUT THEN THE PHONE RINGS..

MARIA - OOOH I BETTER GET THAT
BRAD - YES YOU BETTER

MARIA RUNS TO ANSWER THE PHONE..
BRAD SITS UP AND TAKES A DEEP BREATH AND SEE'S A MAGAZINE SO HE GRABS IT AND
STARTS TO LOOK AT IT…

ABOUT 5 MINUTES PAST, MARIA WALKS BACK OVER TO BRAD.
MARIA - IT WAS MY MOTHER, REMINDING ME ABOUT BAKING WITH HER IN THE
MORNING..

BRAD - OH THAT'S RIGHT YOU HAVE TO GET A EARLY START IN THE MORNING, WELL I
BETTER GET GOING MYSELF.

MARIA - THANK YOU BRAD FOR A GREAT TIME TONIGHT.

BRAD - YOUR WELCOME, GET TOGETHER SOON?

MARIA - OH DEFINITELY.

BRAD AND MARIA HUG AS THEY BOTH WALK TO THE DOOR..

BRAD DRIVES TO HOTEL AND MARIA IS READY FOR BED…

NEXT DAY
BRAD IS AWAKE READY TO START THE DAY, THINKING OF WHAT HE SHOULD DO, SO HE STARTS OFF WITH DRIVING TO A RESTAURANT TO GET A BITE TO EAT..

IN THE MEANTIME MARIA IS READY TO LEAVE TO GO TO HER MOM'S AS SHE IS DRIVING SHE IS THINKING ABOUT BRAD…

MARIA PULLS IN TO HER PARENTS DRIVEWAY, SHE WALKS IN TO HER MOM'S HOUSE..

NOW BRAD IS THINKING ABOUT GOING ON A JOG AT A LOCAL PARK, HE THINK'S ABOUT IT FOR A FEW, THEN DECIDES TO GO BACK TO THE HOTEL TO CHANGE INTO SOME PROPER WORKOUT CLOTHING….

BACK AT MARIA'S PARENT'S HOUSE, MARIA AND MOM ARE LAYING OUT ALL THE BAKING SUPPLIES ON THE TABLE AND COUNTER…

MARIA'S MOM - SO HOW DID YOUR NIGHT GO WITH YOU AND BRAD YESTERDAY?

MARIA - GREAT, HE IS SUCH GOOD COMPANY.

MARIA'S MOM - SO YOU TWO GOING OUT AGAIN?

MARIA - I HOPE SO, BUT I DON'T KNOW WHAT TO ASK HIM TO DO.

MARIA'S MOM - WELL, DON'T YOU HAVE TO HELP TEACH A KID'S JUDO CLASS TOMORROW?

MARIA - YES

MARIA'S MOM - ASK HIM TO COME BY AND WATCH.

MARIA - REALLY? YOU THINK THAT'S A GOOD IDEA..

MARIA'S MOM - YES DEAR I DO.

MARIA - OK, THEN I WILL ASK HIM..

THEY BOTH SMILE, THEN MARIA'S MOM TELL'S HER TO GET THE POWDERED SUGAR OUT, SHE GIGGLES..

AT THE PARK BRAD IS JOGGING, HIS TEXT TONE IS GOING OFF, HE STOPS AND DIGS IN HIS FRONT RIGHT POCKET, HE LOOKS AND SEE'S IT'S MARIA TEXT READS - " HEY WHAT YOU DOING TONIGHT?   AND TOMORROW?

BRAD TEXT - " NO PLANS "

MARIA TEXT - " MEET ME AT PARTON'S RESTAURANT AT 6PM TONIGHT "

BRAD TEXT - " WILL BE THERE "

BRAD IS FINISHING UP HIS JOG HE SEE'S A HOUSE FOR SALE, HE STOPS AND WALKS AROUND THE HOUSE, HE WALKS UP TO THE SIGN WRITES DOWN THE NUMBER, AS HE DRIVES HOME HE DECIDES TO CALL IT, THE REAL ESTATE AGENT ANSWERS THEY BOTH ARE TALKING ABOUT THE HOUSE, SO HE IS SET TO LOOK AT THE SHOWING OF THE HOME TOMORROW WHICH IS A WEDNESDAY AND HE HAS A PLAN WITH MARIA BUT NOT SURE WHAT IT IS YET…

SO BRAD FINISHES THE JOG WITH A SWIFT WALK BACK TO HIS VEHICLE, HE TEXT MARIA BACK AND ASK IF SHE WOULD LIKE TO JOIN HIM FOR A CUP OF TEA OR HOT CHOCOLATE AT A SMALL CORNER CAFÉ " OPEN SEASON'S CAFÉ "
SHE RESPONDS AND SAYS YES, SO BRAD GOES BACK TO HOTEL AND SHOWERS AND DRESSED A LITTLE WARMER BECAUSE OF THE SNOW AND COLDER TEMPERATURES..

MEANWHILE MARIA IS DOING THE SAME THING GETTING READY TO MEET UP WITH BRAD..

TIME GOES BY, BRAD DECIDES TO TEXT MARIA AND SAY'S HE WILL BE BY TO PICK HER UP AT 5P.M.

ABOUT 4:45 P.M. BRAD PULLS UP TO PICK UP MARIA, HE GOES UP TO THE DOOR RINGS THE BELL SHE COMES OUT AND THEY WALK TO THE SUV AND BRAD (AS THE GENTLEMAN HE IS) OPENS THE DOOR FOR MARIA, SHE THANKS HIM…
THEN TALK AS THEN DRIVE A SHORT DISTANCE TO THE CAFÉ..
AS THEY PARK THE WALK IN AND SIT DOWN, THE WAITER HANDS THEM THE MENU, BRAD AND MARIA AGREE THEY WOULD JUST LIKE TO ORDER TWO HOT CHOCOLATES, THE WAITER BRINGS THE DRINK'S TO THEM IN MINUTES… THEN THE CONVERSATION STARTS…

MARIA - SO I WAS GOING TO ASK YOU ABOUT 6   O'CLOCK TOMORROW, THE REASON I WAS WANTING YOU TO STOP BY TO WATCH ME TEACH THE KID'S JUDO CLASS..

BRAD - OH SOUND'S FUN, I HAVEN'T PRACTICE JUDO IN AWHILE..

MARIA - WELL YOU WANT TO SPARE WITH ME, THAT'S IF YOU THINK YOU CAN HANG WITH ME (LAUGHING)

BRAD - YOU JUST GOT YOURSELF A MATCH.

MARIA - GREAT I WILL GO EASY ON YOU.

BRAD - I WOULD APPRECIATE THAT (LAUGHS)

MARIA - HEY UM IF YOU LIKE WE CAN GO DOWN TO THE DOJO AFTER WE LEAVE HERE TO GO PRACTICE BEFORE TOMORROW'S SPARRING MATCH.

BRAD - ISN'T THE SCHOOL CLOSED?

MARIA - YES BUT I GOT A KEY THE OWNER ALWAYS WELCOMES ME TO USE IT ANYTIME I NEED TOO.

BRAD - OK LET'S GO THEN.

MARIA - ALRIGHT.

THE PAIR BOTH FINISHES UP THE DRINKS AND HEADS OUT IN THE SNOW TO WALK TO THE SUV. BUT BEFORE THEY GET IN, MARIA HAPPEN TO SEE THAT THE PET STORE DOWN

THE STREET 3 BUILDINGS FROM THE CAFÉ, IS STILL OPEN..

MARIA - LET'S WALK DOWN TO THE PET STORE

BRAD - SURE

AS THEY WALK, THE SNOW IS COMING DOWN A LITTLE MORE INTENSE AND WIND IS BLOWING.. THEY ENTER THE PET STORE, THE CLERK GREETS THEM,

CLERK - HELLO MARIA, LET ME KNOW IF I CAN HELP YOU WITH ANYTHING

MARIA - THANK YOU BILL.

MARIA KNOW'S ALMOST EVERYONE IN THE TOWN AND ALMOST EVERYONE KNOWS HER..

ALL OF A SUDDEN SHE LOOKS DOWN AT A CAGE AND SEE'S A BEAGLE TYPE BREED PUPPY… HER EYES LIGHT UP AND SMILES..

MARIA - AWWW LOOK AT THIS

BRAD - YES A CUTIE

CLERK - SOMEONE BROUGHT HIM IN YESTERDAY, THE LADY THAT FOUND HIM WANDERING OFF OF OLD ROUTE 40. THE LADY PUT AND ADD IN LOCAL PRESS FOR A MONTH AND NO ONE CLAIMED HIM SO SHE BROUGHT HIM TO ME..

BRAD - MARIA, I THOUGHT YOU WERE ALLERGIC TO DOGS?

MARIA - I WAS THEN I GREW OUT OF IT.

BRAD - GREAT

SO MARIA AND BRAD PETS THE DOG AND PLAYED A LITTLE WITH HIM, THEN SAID THEY'RE GOOD BYE'S TO DOG AND CLERK AND LEAVES TO GO TO THE DOJO…

THEY FINALLY ARRIVE AT THE DOJO MARIA UNLOCKS THE DOOR AND FLIPS THE LIGHTS ON…

BRAD - THIS PLACE LOOKS SO MUCH DIFFERENT SINCE I SAW IT LAST.

MARIA - WELL IT'S ONLY BEEN 30 SOME YEAR BRAD (LAUGH)

BRAD - HAHA, YOUR RIGHT.

THE PLACE IS CLEANED UP AND ALL THE MATS ARE CLEAN AS WELL AND THE PLACE IS ALSO DECORATED WITH CHRISTMAS LIGHTS AND ORNAMENTS..

BRAD AND MARIA STARTS TO PRACTICE, ALL OF A SUDDEN MARIA GRABS BRAD'S ARM AND THROWS HIM OVER HER SHOULDER…

MARIA - YOU OK?

BRAD - YES, WOW YOU STILL GOT IT.

THEY START ROLLING AROUND ON THE MATS AND CATCHING EACH OTHER IN SUBMISSION HOLDS, AS ARM LOCKS, LEG LOCKS, ETC…

AS BRAD AND MARIA FINISHING UP THE JUDO DRILLS, MARIA IS THINKING WHEN BRAD ISN'T EXPECTING, TO TRIP HIM AND HE WILL FALL DOWN… MARIA DECIDES AS THEY ARE WALKING TOWARDS THE WALL WHERE THE CHAIRS ARE, SHE GRABS BRAD AND PUTS HER RIGHT LEG BEHIND HIS LEFT LEG AND WHILE SHE IS HOLDING HIS ARM SHE SPINS HIM AROUND AND TRIPS HIM, AS BRAD LAY'S ON HIS BACK MARIA IS BENDS DOWN AND BRAD GRAB'S MARIA'S ARMS AND PULLS HER ON TOP OF HIM WHEN SHE WASN'T EXPECTING IT..

BRAD - GOT YOU (LAUGHING)

MARIA - I SHOULD HAVE KNOWN

AS THEY BOTH ARE LAYING ON THE FLOOR (THE MATS) BRAD IS LOOKING AT MARIA INTO HER EYES HE TURNS HIS HEAD AND SEE'S THAT THE EXACT LOCATION HE WAS AT IS WHERE HE REALIZED THIS IS WHERE THEY BOTH SAID GOODBYE TO EACH OTHER 30 SOME YEARS AGO AND HE THE MEMORIES RAN THROUGH HIS HEAD WHEN MARIA GAVE HIM THE STUFFED BEAGLE DOG (PATCHES)..
BRAD - MARIA THIS IS THE EXACT PLACE WHERE WE SAID ARE GOODBYE'S.

MARIA - IT IS ISN'T IT.

THEY LOOK AT THE WALL AND THEN BACK AT EACH OTHER LOOKING DEEP INTO EACH OTHER'S EYES, THERE IS A PAUSE, BRAD LOOKS UP TOWARDS THE CEILING AND SEE'S A MISTLETOE…

BRAD - MARIA LOOK.

MARIA - I SEE IT.

THEY BOTH MOVE EACH OTHER'S LIPS CLOSER TO ONE ANOTHER.

BRAD - YOU THINKING WHAT I'M THINKING?

MARIA - YES, AS LONG AS A PHONE DOESN'T RING..

THEY BOTH MOVE IN AND THE VERY FIRST TIME THEY ENGAGE IN A PASSIONATE KISS AND IT LAST FOR SEVERAL MINUTES.

AS THEY KISS THEY BOTH DISENGAGE .

BRAD - I'M SORRY, I, I,

MARIA - YOUR FINE, IT'S OK, I LIKED IT.

BRAD - ME TOO

SO THEY MAKE THEY'RE WAY OFF THE FLOOR AND WALK TOWARDS THE DOOR, MARIA TURNS THE LIGHTS OUT AND LOCKS THE DOOR ON THE WAY OUT…

AS THE TWO WALK TO THE VEHICLE, THEY ARE ALL SMILES, THEY DRIVE OUT OFF THE PARKING LOT ONTO THE STREET, BOTH IN A HAPPY MOOD.

IN THE SUV,

MARIA - AFTER YOU DROP ME OFF AT HOME, REMEMBER WE STILL GOT TO BE AT DOJO BY 6?

BRAD - YES I WILL BE THERE, MATTER OF FACT I'LL BE THERE 10 MINUTES EARLY.

MARIA - SOUNDS LIKE A PLAN.

BRAD DROPS OFF MARIA, AND BEFORE MARIA GETS OUT OF VEHICLE BRAD REACHES OVER AND GIVES HER A QUICK KISS, AFTER THE KISS HE IS GRABBED BY MARIA AND SHE REACHES OVER AND GIVES HIM A KISS…. THEY SAY GOODNIGHT TO EACH OTHER BEFORE MARIA EXIT'S THE VEHICLE….

THE NEXT MORNING BRAD IS IN A HAPPY MOOD, PLAYING MUSIC IN THE HOTEL AND DANCING AROUND SINGING AND FIXING HIM SOME CEREAL AND POURING ORANGE JUICE.. SO HE IS GETTING READY TO GO MEET THE REAL ESTATE AGENT..

HE MEETS THE AGENT AT THE LOCATION WHERE THE HOUSE IS AT, THEY TALK AND GO THROUGH THE HOUSE FOR ABOUT AN HOUR, HE IS HAPPY WITH IT AND THE PRICE.. THE AGENT ASK HIM ABOUT RELOCATION..

AGENT - YOU FROM AROUND HERE ORIGINALLY?

BRAD - YES WHEN I WAS A CHILD, NOW I LIVE IN CALIFORNIA JUST VISITING FRIENDS FOR THE HOLIDAY'S..

AGENT - OH HOW NICE, YOU MOVING BACK HERE TO HARRISONBURG?

BRAD - YOU NEVER KNOW (CHUCKLES)

AGENT - (LAUGHS ALONG)

BRAD SHAKES THE AGENTS HAND AND THEY HIDE TO THE REAL ESTATE OFFICE, AS THE ARRIVE THEY SET DOWN IN THE OFFICE AND BOTH ENGAGE IN A DISCUSSION OF THE SALE…

AFTER ABOUT 45 MINUTES BRAD LEAVES WITH A FOLDER AND A SMILE AS HE ENTERS HIS VEHICLE…

HE ALMOST FORGETS THAT HE HAS TO CALL THE CAR PLACE THAT HE IS RENTING FOR THE 10 DAY'S HE IS IN TOWN….

MEANWHILE MARIA IS RUNNING HER USUAL ERRANDS AND HAS AN APPOINTMENT FOR HAIR, MANICURE AND PEDICURE…..

TIME PASSES AND IT IS CLOSE TO MARIA OF TEACHING THE KIDS CLASS TONIGHT AT 6.. SO SHE GOES HOME AFTER HER APPOINTMENT AT THE SALON, SHE CHANGES CLOTHES AND HEAD ON OVER TO THE DOJO…

BRAD IS LEAVING HIS HOTEL ABOUT THE SAME TIME..

THEY MEET THERE, MARIA UNLOCKS THE DOORS, PARENTS AND THE STUDENTS ARRIVE 12 KIDS SHOW UP SO IT'S A GOOD TURNOUT, MARIA EXPLAINS TO EVERYONE AND

INTRODUCE THAT BRAD WILL BE HELPING OUT WITH SOME OF THE INSTRUCTIONS TODAY…

THE CLASS IS A SUCCESS, BRAD WAS HELPING WITH TAKEDOWNS THE MOST…

SO AS THE CLASS WAS LETTING OUT, IT IS ABOUT 7:15, MARIA ASK BRAD TO THE ANNUAL TOWN CHRISTMAS PARTY AT THE TOWN HALL BUILDING…BRAD ACCEPTS THE INVITE….. BRAD ASK THE DATE OF THE PARTY, IT IS IN TWO DAY'S WHICH IS FRIDAY AT 5 P.M. MARIA TELLS BRAD TO MEET HER AT THE CAFÉ.. BRAD FOLLOWS HER..

AS THEY ENTER THE CAFÉ THE SAME ONE THEY HAD VISITED EARLIER THIS WEEK….

THEY SET DOWN AND ORDER THE SAME DRINKS AS EARLIER THIS WEEK..

BRAD - SO HOW MAY PEOPLE WILL BE THERE/

MARIA - ABOUT 100 OR SO, MAYBE MORE.

BRAD - WOW

MARIA - YEAH I KNOW, THERE IS ALWAYS PLENTY OF FOOD AND DRINKS AND GAMES, MUSIC, GOOD TIME..

BRAD - CAN I ASK YOU IF YOU WOULD BE INTERESTED IN SHOPPING TOMORROW?

MARIA - SURE

BRAD - I NEED TO BUY A FEW THINGS FOR MY RECEPTIONIST AND EVERYONE WORKING IN MY OFFICE..

MARIA - NICE.

THEY FINISH THE DRINKS AND LEAVE THE CAFÉ, THEY WALK OUT TOWARDS THE CARS, THEY BOTH KISS GOODNIGHT AND HUG…

NEXT DAY, AS SOON AS BRAD GETS UP IN THE MORNING, HE IS KINDA IN A HURRY MORE THAN USUAL, AFTER BREAKFAST HE SHOWERS THEN DRESSED AND HEADS OUT.. HE DRIVES TO THE PET STORE, WALKS IN AND TALKS TO THE CLERK (NOT SURE WHAT HE IS TALKING ABOUT)..

MARIA IS CALLING A COUPLE FRIENDS CATCHING UP…. AS SHE IS GETTING READY TO GO SHOPPING LATER WITH BRAD..

HOURS PASS, BRAD CALLS MARIA AND TELLS HER HE IS ON HIS WAY TO PICK HER UP.

HE PULLS IN HER DRIVEWAY AND SHE GETS IN THE PASSENGER SIDE AND THEY ARE ON THE WAY TO THE LOCAL MALL.

THE ARRIVE AT THE MALL AND IN AND OUT OF ABOUT EVERY STORE IN THE MALL, BRAD BUYS A FEW ITEMS AS HE WILL MAKE THEM PRESENTS AND MARIA BUYS A COUPLE AS WELL…. THEY LEAVE THE MALL AND WALK TOWARDS THE SUV AND LOAD THE BACK UP WITH THE ITEMS THEY PURCHASED..

AS THEY ARE DRIVING BACK HOME MARIA SEE'S A CHRISTMAS TUNNEL YOU WALK

THROUGH IN A PLAZA THEY ARE PASSING, SHE INSTANTLY WANTS TO STOP AND GO WALK THROUGH..

BRAD PULLS IN AND THEY RUN OUT OF THE CAR HOLDING HANDS AND WHEN THEY GET TO THE BEGINNING OF THE LIGHTS OF THE TUNNEL THEY STROLL HAND IN HAND AND MARIA LEANING INTO BRAD..

BRAD - I LIKE THIS TOWN

MARIA - ME TOO, I COULDN'T IMAGINE LIVING ANYWHERE ELSE.

BRAD STOPS AND LOOKS AT MARIA..

BRAD - MARIA, I HAVE TO TELL YOU SOMETHING

MARIA - YES BRAD

BRAD - I HAVE BEEN THINKING ABOUT YOU ON AND OFF FOR YEARS AND WHEN I SAW THE STUFFED DOG YOU GAVE ME, I REALLY WAS THINKING OF YOU A LOT AND WANTED TO AT LEAST SEE HOW YOU HAVE BEEN AND WHERE YOU WAS AT IN LIFE, THIS HAPPENED SO FAST, AND IT FEELS RIGHT, I REALLY LIKE BEING AROUND YOU, I NEVER FELT THIS WAY ABOUT A GIRL IN MY WHOLE LIFE, AND YOUR KISS, WELL IT WAS SO NICE AND I FELT SOMETHING INSIDE AND IT FELT GOOD....I HAD TO GET THIS OFF MY CHEST..

MARIA - BRAD I FEEL THE SAME WAY, AND I KNOW YOU WILL BE LEAVING IN A COUPLE DAY'S AND NOT KNOWING WHEN WE WILL SEE EACH OTHER AGAIN… LETS JUST MAKE THE BEST OF WHAT WE GOT GOING ON NOW AND NOW SLOW DOWN WHAT TIME WE GOT LEFT BEFORE YOU LEAVE..

BRAD - YOUR RIGHT LETS FINISH THIS WALK AND CAN'T WAIT TILL THE PARTY TOMORROW EVENING….

THEY WALK GAZING AT THE PRETTY LIGHTS… AS THEY FINISH THE WALK THEY BOTH HEAD BACK TO THE CAR HOLDING HANDS..

AS THEY ARE DRIVING THEY ARE HOLDING HANDS STILL…

HE DROPS MARIA OFF AT HER HOUSE ENDING THE GREAT NIGHT..

NEXT DAY, BRAD IS EXITED ABOUT THE CHRISTMAS PARTY TONIGHT, HE GOES TO THE STORE TO PICK UP SOME PIES AND COOKIES TO TAKE TO THE EVENT..

HE ENDS UP PURCHASING 3 PIES AND 4 BOX OF HOLIDAY COOKIES..

AS THE DAY IS COMING TO AN END, MARIA IS AT THE TOWN HALL PUTTING SOME FINAL TOUCHES ON THE TABLES AND WALLS AND MAKING SURE THERE WILL BE ENOUGH PLATES FOR EVERYONE.. THE FOOD IS BEING COOKED AS WE SPEAK AND KEEPING WARM THE DRINKS ARE READY THE DJ ARRIVES AND SETTING UP…

MARIA TEXT BRAD TO TELL HIM IF HE LIKES HE CAN COME AND HELP SET UP WITH SOME THINGS, SO BRAD DOESN'T THINK TWICE HE PUTS THE PIES AND COOKIES IN THE VEHICLE AND JETS OFF TO THE PARTY…

BRAD ARRIVES AND IMMEDIATELY HELPS MARIA AND OTHERS THERE, AND SETS THE TABLES....

FINALLY TIME ROLLS AROUND EVERYONE STARTS TO POUR IN THE DOORS AND THE PARTY STARTS, BRAD GETS TO MEET AND TALK TO ALL THE LOCAL PEOPLE AND MEETS MARIA'S FRIENDS AND PARENTS AGAIN... THEY ARE DANCING TOGETHER AND LAUGHING....

5 HOURS LATER EVERYONE THINS OUT AND BRAD AND MARIA AND A FEW OTHERS CLEAN UP, AND MARIA KNOWS IT'S BRAD'S LAST DAY HERE BEFORE HE HAS TO GO BACK HOME TO THE WEST COAST, THEY BOTH LEARNED SO MUCH ABOUT EACH OTHER IN JUST A WEEKS TIME....BRAD SEEMS LIKE HE IS ANXIOUS TO TELL MARIA SOMETHING..

THEY FINISH CLEANING THE TOWN HALL AND BOTH LEAVE OUT THE DOOR, MARIA TURNS THE LIGHTS OFF...

THEY BOTH WALK OUT TO THE PARKING LOT, THEY ARE STANDING CLOSE..

MARIA - WELL I GUESS YOUR LEAVING TOMORROW MORNING

BRAD - YES

MARIA - WHEN YOU THINK YOU COME BACK TO VISIT?

BRAD - SOON, HEY COME WITH ME, HOP IN THE CAR

BRAD DRIVES TO THE HOUSE HE WAS LOOKING AT A COUPLE DAYS BACK.,

THEY PULL UP THE BOTH EXIT THE CAR,,

MARIA - WHAT'S GOING ON?

BRAD RUNS OVER TO MARIA GRABS HER HAND AND THEY BOTH WALK FAST TO THE HOUSE HE UNLOCKS THE DOOR THEY BOTH WALK IN...

BRAD - MARIA, THIS IS NOW MY HOUSE

MARIA - WHAT?

BRAD - I AM BOUGHT THIS HOUSE SO I CAN BE HERE WITH YOU MORE

MARIA - BRAD, WHAT ABOUT YOU JOB IN CALIFORNIA?

BRAD - I GOT THAT COVERED, I WAS TALKING TO SOME LOCAL PEOPLE HERE ON AND OFF SINCE I HAVE BEEN HERE AND THEY NEED A GOOD ATTORNEY IN TOWN, SO I AM OPENING UP AN OFFICE HERE IN TOWN...

MARIA - I AM SO SURPRISED

SHE HUGS BRAD TIGHT WITH TEARS OF JOY IN HER EYES

BRAD - ANOTHER THING, MY PARENTS ARE FLYING IN AFTER NEW YEARS AND I AM COMING ALONG MY DAD IS RETIRED SO THEY WANT TO LOOK AT HOUSES HERE AS WELL.

MARIA - THIS IS SO GREAT, I AM SO HAPPY, BUT YOU HAVE YOUR OFFICE ESTABLISHED

FOR YEAR IN CALIFORNIA.

BRAD - I'M STILL GOING TO WORK THERE TOO, IT WILL EVEN OUT, TRUST ME I GOT IT
COVERED.. THAT'S WHAT JETS ARE FOR..

BRAD - MARIA, I GOT ONE MORE SURPRISE..

BRAD WAVES FOR A GENTLEMAN IN A VAN SITTING IN FRONT OF THE HOUSE, THE MAN
GETS OUT AND SHE SEE'S IT'S THE OWNER OF THE LOCAL PET SHOP, HE OPENS THE BACK
DOORS OF THE VAN.. BRAD GRABS MARIA'S HAND THEY WALK CLOSER ALL OF A
SUDDEN SHE SEE'S THE DOG SHE WAS VISITING DAY'S AGO THE STRAY BEAGLE SHE
BENDS TO HER KNEES AND HUGS THE DOG....

MARIA GETS BACK UP AND HUGS THE PET STORE OWNER AND THEN BRAD

MARIA - THANK YOU SO MUCH AS SHE IS CRYING

BRAD - THIS IS YOUR DOG NOW MARIA, MERRY CHRISTMAS

MARIA HUGS AND KISSES BRAD.. MERRY CHRISTMAS TO YOU..

BRAD - SO WHAT YOU GOING TO NAME HIM?

MARIA LOOKS AT BRAD SMILES BEND BACK DOWN TO HUG THE DOG..

MARIA - I WILL NAME HIM " PATCHES "

NOW THE PET STORE OWNER WISHES THEM A MERRY CHRISTMAS AND DRIVES OFF
MARIA, BRAD AND THE DOG ARE IN THE FRONT YARD OF THE NEW HOUSE HUGGING
CRYING AND LAUGHING...

THE JOURNEY FOR BRAD AND MARIA WAS A SUCCESS AND THEY BOTH ARE HAPPY,
LOOKS LIKE A PROMISING FUTURE FOR THE COUPLE AND PATCHES......

THE END

STORY BY DANIEL A. BROCK